THE TECHNOLOGY OF
BASKETBALL

by Suzanne Slade

HIGH-TECH SPORTS

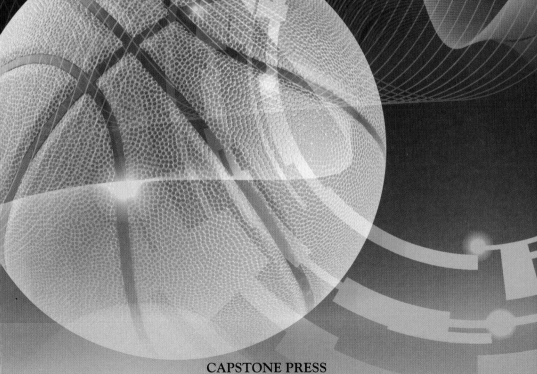

CAPSTONE PRESS
a capstone imprint

Sports Illustrated Kids High-Tech Sports are published by Capstone Press,
1710 Roe Crest Drive, North Mankato, Minnesota 56003
www.capstonepub.com

SI Kids is a trademark of Time Inc. Used with permission.

Library of Congress Cataloging-in-Publication Data
Slade, Suzanne.
  The technology of basketball / by Suzanne Slade.
     p. cm.—(Sports illustrated kids. High-tech sports)
  Includes bibliographical references and index.
  Summary: "Discusses the forms of technology that has revolutionized the game of basketball"
—Provided by publisher.
  ISBN 978-1-4296-9956-3 (library binding)
  ISBN 978-1-62065-908-3 (paperback)
1. Basketball—Juvenile literature. I. Title.
  GV885.1.S524 2013
  796.323--dc23   2012033675

Editorial Credits
Anthony Wacholtz, editor; Veronica Scott and Sarah Bennett, designers; Eric Gohl, media researcher;
Eric Manske, production specialist

Photo Credits
Alamy: PhotoStock-Israel, 13; AP Images: Andy Manis, 23, Greg Campbell, 25, Rajah
Bose, 28; Courtesy of 94Fifty Sports Technologies: 6, 7; Courtesy of Airborne Athletics,
Inc.: 8, 9; Getty Images: AFP/Roslan Rahman, 11, NBAE/Andrew D. Bernstein, 42,
NBAE/Fernando Medina, 19, NBAE/Gary Dineen, 4, NBAE/Issac Baldizon, 16, NBAE/
Layne Murdoch, 45; Newscom: Cal Sport Media/Chris Szagola, 18, Getty Images/AFP/
Teh Eng Koon, 44, KRT/Sleets, Geib, 29, MCT/Michael Laughlin, 37, Reuters/Lucy
Nicholson, 15, Reuters/Rebecca Cook, 39, UPI/Brian Kersey, 38, www.isiphotos.com/
Michael Pimentel, 22; Northwestern Lake Forest Hospital: 27; Shutterstock: Chimpinski,
cover (background, ball), 1, Maxene Huiyu, 24, ssuaphotos, cover (background, basket);
Sports Illustrated: Bill Frakes, 17, David E. Klutho, 34, John Biever, 21 (right), 31, 32–33,
John W. McDonough, cover, 5, 14, 20, 26, 33 (right), 35, 40, 41, Manny Millan, 10, 21
(left & middle), Peter Read Miller, 12, Robert Beck, 30, 36
Design Elements: Shutterstock

Printed in the United States of America in Stevens Point, Wisconsin

TABLE OF CONTENTS

BEATING THE BUZZER

As Chicago Bulls guard Derrick Rose dribbled down the court, everyone in the Bradley Center was on their feet. The Bulls were tied with the Milwaukee Bucks at 104 points each. As the last seconds of the March 7, 2012, game ticked away, Rose put up a shot in front of Bucks guard Brandon Jennings. All eyes were fixed on the net as the buzzer sounded. Swish! The fans went crazy. Because it was a close play, three officials huddled around the replay screen. After looking at the replay, the officials made their decision: Rose beat the buzzer. The Bulls won!

◀ Derrick Rose

For more than a century, players and fans have enjoyed the great game of basketball. Through the years the high-action sport has basically remained the same. Well-executed plays, quick ball handling, and precise shooting are still key to a successful game. Fans continue to go wild over killer crossovers, high-flying slam dunks, and last-second, game-winning baskets.

But recent technologies have redefined how players train, the type of equipment they use, and how the game is called by officials. Now "intelligent" basketballs instruct players, shoes help players leap higher, and electronic scoreboards do a whole lot more than give the score. Engineering breakthroughs have given fans new ways to view the game they love. There's no doubt, technology is taking the sport of basketball to new and exciting heights.

LeBron James of the Miami Heat soars for a spectacular dunk.

FACT

James Naismith, a physical education teacher in Massachusetts, invented the game of basketball in 1891 to keep his students busy during the cold winter months. Some of basketball's rules came from a game Naismith played as a child called "Duck on a Rock."

CHAPTER 1

SMART BASKETBALLS

How do the top pro players develop perfect shots? Lots of practice, of course! They also listen to coaches who carefully study every part of their shots—ball spin, height, and release. That's how they learn what works and what doesn't.

Now a "smart" basketball can tell players what they're doing wrong. The special ball has a small circuit board mounted inside. The circuit board is made of tiny **accelerometers** and **gyroscopes** that weigh only 5 grams (about the weight of five paper clips), so its weight doesn't change the ball's bounce or flight.

> **accelerometer**—a piece of equipment that measures acceleration
> **gyroscope**—a device that contains a spinning wheel that is used to measure direction of motion

During practice drills, the smart ball records every movement—its speed, direction, and turns. The data is sent through wireless sensors to a computer where it is analyzed to determine how the player handles and shoots the ball. Then it gives a detailed breakdown of each dribble and shot. With this information, players know exactly what to work on.

A basketball program from 94Fifty can track the development of players' skills.

FACT

The recommended pressure for most basketballs is between 7 and 9 pounds per square inch (PSI). The NBA requires all game balls to be inflated between $7\frac{1}{2}$ and $8\frac{1}{2}$ PSI. WNBA balls have an air pressure limit of 9 PSI.

BASKETBALL SHOOTING MACHINE

A busy basketball coach can always use a good assistant. Basketball shooting machines are hard-working assistants that never need to stop and rest. Shooting machines are used in school, college, and professional practices around the country.

These high-tech machines are placed under a basket where they catch shots and throw the ball back to players. They also run practice drills such as rebounding, shooting from the perimeter, and defensive training drills.

A basketball shooting machine lobs a shot toward the basket during a defensive training exercise.

Basketball shooting machines can also be programmed to manage customized practices. They toss balls to players at a certain velocity and rotation speed. With the machine, players can practice receiving bounce passes, skip passes, lob passes, or hard chest passes. Another bonus feature is the basketball machine can store individual information about every player, so it provides each one with individualized practice on his or her weaknesses. The wireless remote allows coaches to start new drills or change any features of the drill such as ball speed or rotation with one click of a button.

THE HEART OF THE GAME

Players' muscles work hard during a game. The hardest working muscle of all may be the heart. The heart pumps blood, which carries nutrients and oxygen, throughout the body. In 1993 the world of basketball was shocked when 27-year-old Reggie Lewis, captain of the Boston Celtics, died of a heart attack. People wondered if the tragedy could have been prevented. Now professional players are required to have medical screenings to discover possible heart problems.

Reggie Lewis played for the Boston Celtics for six seasons before suffering a heart attack.

Many pro teams bring cutting-edge medical technology into their training rooms to do heart exams. They conduct routine **cardiac** stress tests to see how well a player's heart is functioning. Some teams take three-dimensional images of players' hearts. Other tests might include a wireless **electrocardiogram** (EKG), which finds problems in the electrical signals the heart sends to contract its muscles and pump blood. While testing helps find possible life-threatening conditions, it's also useful to find out how quickly a player's heart rate recovers after a hard practice.

Some smartphones come with a built-in EKG, allowing people to check for abnormal heart rhythms wherever they go.

FACT

Sessoter Ikpah loved playing for the American International College basketball team in Springfield, Massachusetts. But when doctors discovered he had a serious heart defect, Sesso thought his basketball career was over. Then Dr. Francis Marchlinski suggested an experimental **defibrillator** that was stronger than a traditional one. Sesso decided to have the new defibrillator implanted in 2010. The defibrillator was placed under Sesso's skin, on top of his collarbone. It can detect an irregular heartbeat and even give the heart a small shock to get it back into rhythm. With the new defibrillator in place, Sesso was soon back on the court!

cardiac—something that relates to the heart
electrocardiogram (EKG)—a recording of the electrical activity of the heart
defibrillator—a machine that applies an electric current to the heart

CUSTOMIZED WORKOUT

Players often set personal goals for each workout. Goals may change depending on injuries, the player's physical condition, or the length of time before the next game. But it's not always easy for trainers and coaches to see if players are doing their best in a workout. The amount of sweat and number of baskets don't tell the whole story. But new technology can reveal who's slacking off and who's working hard.

Carmelo Anthony works out with a personal trainer, using drills to focus on specific abilities such as driving.

Players on some teams wear heart-rate belts during practice. The belts send data, such as heartbeats per minute, to a courtside computer through its antenna. Trainers wear small, watchlike computers on their wrists with baseline, preseason data on each player. The trainers compare players' preseason data with their current heart rates. Based on a scale from one to five, the information shows how hard each player worked during practice. Trainers then determine if workout goals were met. If not, a player may add a few laps around the court to his or her workout.

Personal heart rate monitors help trainers and coaches track the athletes' health when they play.

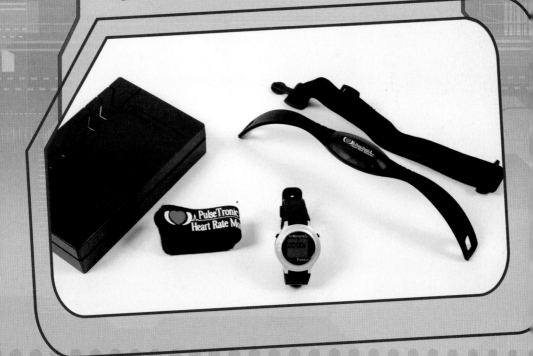

CHAPTER 2

HIGH-FLYING SHOES

When you think high-tech, you might not think shoes. But compared to the first basketball shoes, which had heavy rubber soles and thick canvas tops, today's light, breathable shoes seem like scientific marvels. And they continue to get better. A player's shoes can add a few inches to his or her jump. Those inches are just what some players need to make a slam dunk!

◄ Kevin Love

Shoes support low arches, cushion feet from hard surfaces, and keep feet dry. But can they help you jump higher? That's what the makers of new "propulsion" basketball shoes are saying. Here's how they work: A cushiony "launch pad" in the front of the shoe compresses when a player steps down, preparing to jump. The compression stores some of the player's downward force, which is released as upward force when a player starts to jump, pushing the player up a little higher. One shoe company claims its high-jumping shoes help players leap up to 3½ inches (9 centimeters) higher than regular shoes.

The NBA has banned players from using certain equipment, such as Concept 1 propulsion shoes (above). The league doesn't want players to have an advantage over other players because of equipment.

FACT

The average NBA player can jump about 28 inches (71 cm) off the ground.

SHOE GRIP

Basketball players move fast. They need to change direction on a dime. To do that, a player's shoes must have good traction. But dust and worn-out playing surfaces on indoor courts can make shoes slip.

To get better traction, players sometimes spit on their hands and wipe down their shoes. They also wipe their shoes on pads on the sidelines to clean them off. These simple tricks help for awhile, but the increased traction doesn't last long. New nonslip "grip liquid" products give shoes maximum traction on smooth wood floors to help athletes play their best game.

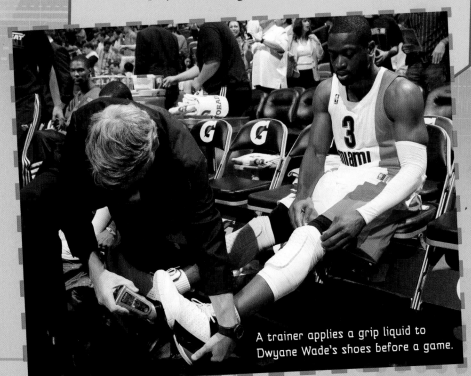

A trainer applies a grip liquid to Dwyane Wade's shoes before a game.

The grip liquid is applied to shoes through a sponge on top of a bottle. Manufacturers say the special formula is pressure sensitive. That means as shoe pressure on the court increases, shoe traction increases. The product dries fast and may need to be applied several times during a game to give the best traction. When shoes don't slip, players have fewer injuries and more confidence on the court.

The grip liquid helps players change direction or cut to the basket.

HAND GRIP

In the high-energy game of basketball, it's no surprise players sweat. Wet, sweaty hands can lead to a slippery grip and bad passes, missed baskets, and dropped balls. To avoid these problems, players have tried using a powdery chalk on their hands. But after awhile the chalk dust mixes with the sweat and creates messy, sticky hands.

Kevin Garnett slaps his hands together, sending up a cloud of chalk during his pregame ritual.

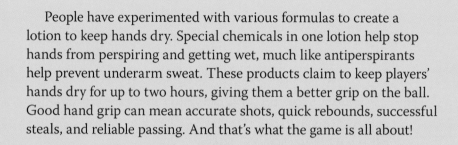

People have experimented with various formulas to create a lotion to keep hands dry. Special chemicals in one lotion help stop hands from perspiring and getting wet, much like antiperspirants help prevent underarm sweat. These products claim to keep players' hands dry for up to two hours, giving them a better grip on the ball. Good hand grip can mean accurate shots, quick rebounds, successful steals, and reliable passing. And that's what the game is all about!

Dwight Howard applies hand grip before the tip off.

THE UNIFORM

Chris Paul ▶

A basketball uniform not only looks good, it's also an important part of the game. Scientists are working to discover ways to make uniforms perform better. For example, the 2010 NBA uniforms were 30 percent lighter than in past years and dried twice as fast as the previous ones.

A clothing designer worked with the NBA for four years to test the uniforms' performance and comfort. More than 200 NBA players tried out the experimental clothing during practice and games. Researchers studied the uniforms' performance and listened to the players' feedback.

Made from 60 percent recycled materials, the new uniforms have fewer seams and less friction between the garment and the players' skin. The shirt weight was reduced by using numbers on the back made from breathable mesh instead of the old heavier, dense materials. The specially designed fabric absorbed moisture in less than three seconds, which kept players dryer and cooler.

FACT

Basketball shorts were rather short until 1984. That year Chicago Bulls legend Michael Jordan asked for longer ones. The idea caught on and other teams followed the longer design.

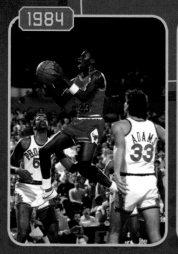

1984

1994

2012

CHAPTER 3

PLAYER TRACKING SYSTEM

During a basketball game, there's a lot of fast-moving action. New **high-definition (HD)** cameras capture every move of the players, the ball, and even the referees. Using virtual dots on the ball, as well as players' and referees' heads, a series of specially placed cameras record all the details. The data can show if the referees' calls are accurate by revealing where the refs were when they made their calls and how fast they followed the action.

Referees' calls don't always sit well with the players.

Coaches are more interested in using the tracking system to look at players' performance. The tracking system breaks down part of a play, allowing coaches to look beyond obvious moves like a block or steal. Now they can compare how effective various guards are against the same player. The coaches look for smaller moves, such as how close one of the guards stayed to the player he or she was defending. Or they can analyze offensive plays by the speed of passes and the height and angle of shots. With this detailed data, coaches have even more information to help players become their best.

One tracking system contains a camera, a computer, and a speaker. The camera records details of the athlete's movements. The computer analyzes the data, and the speaker announces instructions on how to change the form for better results.

high definition (HD)—a quality of displaying videos or pictures with a high resolution to create a sharper image

BASKETBALL SIMULATION DRILLS

In a game where split-second decisions can make or break a play, players need to think fast on their feet. For years computer **simulation** has trained people for activities that require fast thinking, such as piloting a plane or working in space. Now basketball players can hone their decision-making skills with simulation too. Many college teams are taking advantage of this technology by giving their players basketball simulation games.

Simulation is a useful training tool for many activities. Flight simulators allow pilots to train without taking to the skies.

simulation—a computer model of something in real life

Played on a computer, basketball simulation games are a workout for the brain. A practice session lasts about 30 minutes, and the manufacturer recommends players practice one to three sessions each week. When creating the game, developers thought about the brain skills basketball players use most, such as positioning, reading plays, and performing under pressure. Then they designed a system to simulate these same skills on a screen. Each player's individual program can be changed to improve his or her weak areas. So players can improve their game without even breaking a sweat!

A college student uses a program called The Basketball IntelliGym to improve his reflexes and decision-making skills on the court.

GAME TIME

CHAPTER 4

STAYING STRONG

Basketball players do a lot of running and jumping, which are hard on the knees. One of the most common injuries players face is knee **cartilage** damage. Damaged or missing cartilage causes joint pain and can lead to the loss of the entire knee joint.

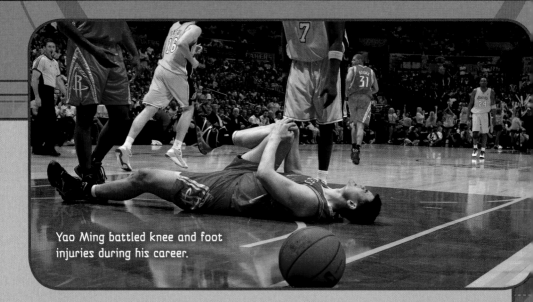

Yao Ming battled knee and foot injuries during his career.

But what if doctors could **clone** a player's knee cartilage and replace the damaged cartilage with brand new tissue? Doctors in the field of tissue engineering are doing just that. In a procedure called an autologous chondrocyte implantation (ACI), doctors remove a small piece of knee cartilage from the damaged knee. The cartilage is cloned in a lab where millions of new cells are grown for four to six weeks. The new tissue is reinserted into the knee, where it slowly connects to bone in the knee joint. Although this procedure was developed recently, it has promise to help many basketball players return to peak performance.

cartilage—the soft tissue that cushions joints
clone—to create cells that are exact copies of existing cells

A NEW KNEE?

In her senior year of high school, Brooke Evans earned a scholarship to play college basketball. But she also started having knee problems. "Whenever I would play, I would feel severe pain in my knee and sometimes the knee would give out," Brooke explained. When her surgeon discovered a problem with cartilage in her knee, Brooke began to worry about her athletic future. Then the surgeon recommended an ACI. After the procedure, she went through physical therapy and red-shirted her freshman year in college. Brooke was back on the court her sophomore year. "This year I was able to play and practice just like everyone else," Brooke said.

Dr. Roger Chams and Brooke Evans

DUNK-PROOF GLASS

In the past a slam dunk could cause the backboard to shatter. A shattered board often meant a delayed or canceled game, or even injuries. In 1967 the NCAA decided to take action and banned dunking for about 10 years.

Players scattered after a backboard-shattering dunk by Gonzaga's Bol Kong in 2009.

But thanks to technology, glass backboards are more stable, and the dunk is back to stay. New glass backboards are heated to a certain temperature where the glass becomes soft. Then the glass is cooled quickly. This temperature cycling creates tempered glass that is four to five times stronger than the glass once used for backboards.

Breakaway rims also prevent shattered boards by allowing the basketball rim to bend when a player grabs it during a shot. A breakaway rim absorbs the downward force of the player's hand. This prevents tension on the backboard, which could set off a series of fast-moving cracks and big trouble!

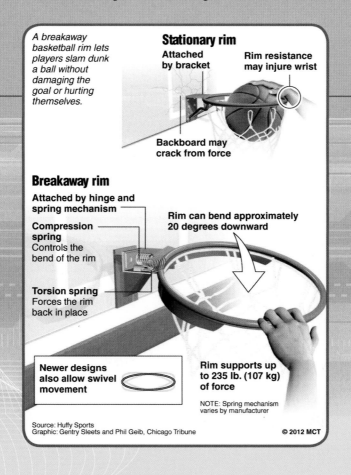

A breakaway basketball rim lets players slam dunk a ball without damaging the goal or hurting themselves.

Stationary rim

Attached by bracket

Rim resistance may injure wrist

Backboard may crack from force

Breakaway rim

Attached by hinge and spring mechanism

Compression spring
Controls the bend of the rim

Torsion spring
Forces the rim back in place

Rim can bend approximately 20 degrees downward

Newer designs also allow swivel movement

Rim supports up to 235 lb. (107 kg) of force

NOTE: Spring mechanism varies by manufacturer

Source: Huffy Sports
Graphic: Gentry Sleets and Phil Geib, Chicago Tribune

© 2012 MCT

FACT

A crack travels about 3,400 miles (5,470 kilometers) per hour through glass. So a crack moves across an entire backboard in 0.001 seconds!

PLAY IT AGAIN

Referees can't see all the action all the time. One wrong call can be the difference between a big win and a disappointing loss. Fortunately, some refs have instant replay equipment to help them out. State-of-the-art cameras around the court record the game from many angles. Nearby screens instantly replay the action from various viewpoints.

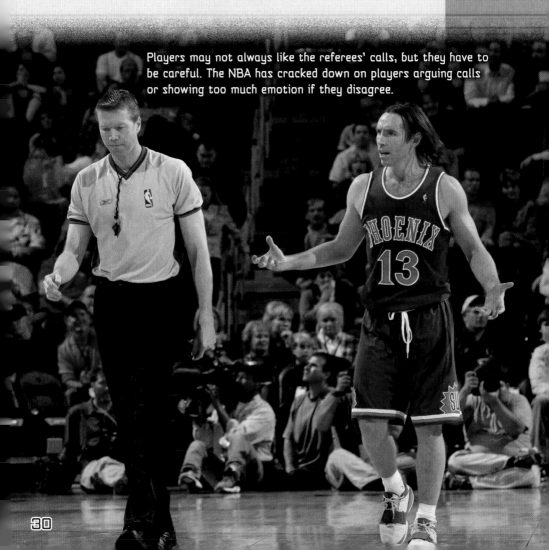

Players may not always like the referees' calls, but they have to be careful. The NBA has cracked down on players arguing calls or showing too much emotion if they disagree.

But refs can't use video footage for every call. The NBA, WNBA, NCAA, and other basketball organizations have rules about when refs can use instant replays. Refs use instant replay in specific game situations, such as when a foul is committed or a basket is made at the end of a period. But even then, refs have a limited amount of time to review the video.

Replay technology has helped refs make more good calls in the past, and it may play an even bigger role in the future. The NCAA rules committee is considering allowing more instant replays in the last minute of a college game. Some basketball fans are hoping the NCAA will adopt a "challenge system," which would allow coaches to ask refs to review game footage on questionable calls. As technology changes, there's no doubt the way we use it will continue to change too.

BEATING THE LIGHT

There's nothing more exciting than a buzzer-beating shot at the end of a close game. But how can the referee know if the ball left the player's hands in time? Technology to the rescue!

◄ A red LED strip lights up when the shot clock reaches zero.

NBA players have 24 seconds to attempt a basket (and at least hit the rim) after taking possession of the ball. For players in the NCAA, the time to beat is 35 seconds. After that, the shot clock light and the buzzer announce that it's too late! Most backboards have a special light that turns on when the shot clock expires. The shot clock light is usually a red LED (Light-Emitting Diodes) strip that runs around the edge of the glass backboard. Referees watch to see if the light turns on before the ball leaves the player's hands. On really close calls, they can double-check a replay to know what happened first, the release or the light.

FACT

The shot clock was invented by Danny Biasone, owner of the Syracuse Nationals. He came up with the idea after the 1953–54 season to help speed up the game. The NBA's first president, Maurice Podoloff, said, "The adoption of the clock was the most important event in the NBA."

NUMBERS GAME

Many cameras capture the action of regular-season games, but even more cameras are used during the playoffs. Dozens of computer systems are needed to record every detail. Manned by well-trained statisticians, computers track up to 500 events, such as shot attempts, points scored, blocks, turnovers, and three-point attempts. Statisticians record each stat using a mix of touchscreen and keyboard entry. The thousands of stats the computer systems track are sent to a powerful server hidden behind the stands.

A camera suspended above the court shows an overhead view of the game. The camera travels along wires to keep up with the action.

Video capture technologies have started taking over some of the tiresome data-tracking work. Video capture technology includes cameras that are programmed to recognize and record specific player moves on their own. With this additional help, experts say statisticians will have extra time to record even more stats.

Cameras are positioned behind the backboards to provide a unique angle of every shot and rebound.

CHAPTER 5

THE SCORE AND MORE

Basketball scoreboards provide much more than the score. They're huge entertainment centers in the middle of the arena where all the fans can see them. HD scoreboards get fans pumped up before the game begins with pregame videos or highlight reels from earlier games. Throughout the game the scoreboards display individual player stats, player interviews, and advertisements. They provide slow-motion replays of close calls, thrown elbows, and last-second, game-winning shots. Scoreboards also show live video of fans at the game, entertainment during timeouts and halftime, and upcoming events.

The huge eight-sided scoreboard at the Staples Center ensures Lakers and Clippers fans never miss a moment of the game.

Lit with thousands of LED lights, side-by-side scoreboard screens have crisp graphics fans can view from many angles. This wireless board receives scores and other data through its antenna from control panels on the sidelines. Some teams purchase add-on scoreboard features that automatically update their websites and other social media with the latest scores. With new, high-tech scoreboards, there's never a break in the action!

SUPER SCOREBOARD

One of the biggest scoreboards in the NBA is found in the Chesapeake Energy Arena in Oklahoma City. Weighing more than 23 tons (21 metric tons), the super-sized scoreboard measures 31 X 35 feet (9 X 11 meters). Equipped with cutting-edge graphics, the system includes 12 video panels. Two unique video panels at the bottom tilt in a V-shape so Oklahoma City Thunder fans in the first rows can see the scoreboard too. The total cost for this impressive fan experience was almost $4 million!

FACT

LED lights last 50 to 100 times longer than the standard incandescent bulbs used in earlier scoreboards. Incandescent bulbs waste energy by emitting heat and light wavelengths that human eyes can't detect.

SECURITY

Fans have a great time watching their favorite players at NBA, WNBA, and NCAA games. To keep fans and players safe, specially trained security departments use advanced cameras and metal detectors, along with detailed security plans.

Using a handheld metal detector, a security guard scans a fan entering the United Center in Chicago before a Bulls game.

Before a game even begins, surveillance cameras comb the parking lots for trouble. Walk-through metal detectors and handheld detectors prevent people from bringing dangerous items into the arenas. Cameras monitor the crowd for potentially threatening activities. Many cameras have remote-control access, so security workers can move cameras and zoom in and out.

Security guards at professional basketball games can be assisted by local police officers if fans become unruly.

Arenas with surveillance systems stream live crowd video footage over the Internet to security team members in remote sites. Some sports centers, such as the Wells Fargo Center in Philadelphia, Pennsylvania, ask fans to be on the lookout for trouble. They provide a "tattle texting" number so fans can anonymously report suspicious-looking activity.

THE CROWD GOES WILD

With interactive crowd technology, fans aren't just spectators—they're part of the action. A series of eight HD cameras with motion-tracking systems are mounted on arena scoreboards or rafters. They capture the movements of the crowd and send them to a powerful server, which translates their movements into a response. This allows fans to interact with game sponsors, the team, and even each other.

The scoreboard screen might ask fans to wave their arms to the right to select an option in a sponsor poll. With a wave of their arms, fans can choose the song they'd like played next or answer trivia questions. Interactive cameras can detect motion in various parts of the arena. One section of the stands can compete with another in a game shown on the scoreboard's screens.

Many fans will cheer, dance, and hold up catchy signs to appear on the giant screens at a pro basketball game.

GAME ON THE GO

Fans can follow their favorite teams with hundreds of basketball **apps** for mobile devices. Apps are created by programmers who write lines of code with a programming language. Each line of the code gives a certain instruction. When all the lines work together, they perform the function of the app.

Kobe Bryant (from left), Dirk Nowitzki, and Carlos Boozer watch a video on an iPhone before an All-Star practice.

app—software that runs on mobile handheld devices and performs a specific task; app is short for application

There are lots of apps to choose from. Some you pay for, and others are free. Popular apps display live game action or radio broadcasts of games. For those new to the game of basketball, apps provide game rules and explanations of referee signals. Serious fans might want an app to track the stats of their favorite players. There are also chat room apps where people can talk to other fans of their favorite team. With all the apps on the market, people can keep up with team schedules, standings, and the latest scores no matter where they go.

More and More Apps

The number of apps has skyrocketed in recent years. No matter what your interest, you can find an app for almost every sport, hobby, or subject.

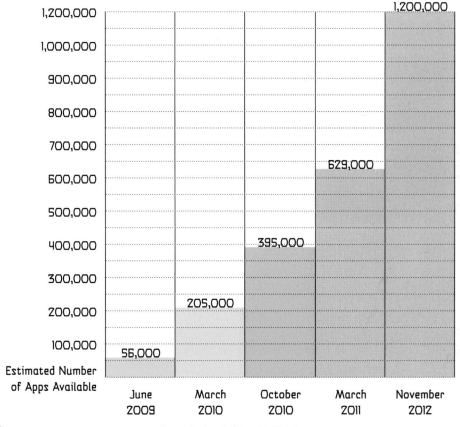

Sources: Business Insider and Mobilewalla

WATCHING AROUND THE WORLD

State-of-the-art equipment and advances in communication are bringing basketball to enthusiastic fans across the globe. In fact, NBA finals and NCAA Final Four games have been transmitted to more than 200 countries, including China, France, India, Australia, Japan, and the United Kingdom.

NBA fans in Beijing, China, watch a game on a projector screen between the Houston Rockets and Milwaukee Bucks.

Fans in some parts of the world can watch games live by streaming over the Internet. They can buy tickets to viewing areas in movie theaters and arenas to watch games, sometimes in 3D. Most of the games are live, while others are replays because of time zone differences. Many games transmitted overseas have onsite sports announcers who provide live game commentary. Commercials during timeouts often feature local stores and businesses. Thanks to technology, fans can feel as if they have a courtside seat, even though they are thousands of miles away from the action.

THE SECRET OF 3D

A 3D game experience begins with the right equipment. That includes six HD camera systems, each with two side-by-side cameras and special HD lenses. In each of the six systems, one camera focuses on the up-close game action, while the other pans back and films the depth of the court. The camera feeds are sent through special cables that can carry large amounts of data to a production truck outside. The truck contains a switcher that combines the close-up and far-away camera shots. The video is then sent to the viewing area.

A theater in Dallas, Texas, hosted a 3D event featuring a game between the Dallas Mavericks and the Los Angeles Clippers.

Fans wear special glasses that simulate the way our eyes normally see depth. Adult eyes are about 2 inches (5 cm) apart. When a fan looks at a basketball player, he sees the player from two slightly different angles. The brain combines these two images together to detect distance and depth. A 3D video of a game projects the court from two different angles and in two colors, usually red and blue. The lens in a pair of 3D glasses have different colored filters (red and blue) that separate the game footage into two images so each eye sees only one. The brain combines the two pictures into one, giving the video depth, which means exciting 3D action!

GLOSSARY

accelerometer—a piece of equipment that measures acceleration

app—software that runs on mobile handheld devices and performs a specific task; app is short for application

cardiac—something that relates to the heart

cartilage—the soft tissue that cushions joints

clone—to create cells that are exact copies of existing cells

compress—squeeze down into a smaller space

defibrillator—a machine that applies an electric current to the heart

electrocardiogram (EKG)—a recording of the electrical activity of the heart

friction—the resistance caused by one surface moving over another surface

gyroscope—a device that contains a spinning wheel that is used to measure direction of motion

high definition (HD)—equipment that captures and displays videos or pictures with a high resolution to create a sharper image

incandescent bulb—a bulb that lights up when electricity heats its filament causing it to glow

programming language—an artificial language created to give instructions to a machine such as a computer

simulation—a computer model of something in real life

tempered glass—glass that has been heated and cooled in a specific way to make it more resistant to breaking

traction—the amount of grip one surface has while moving over another surface

velocity—the speed an object travels in a certain direction

READ MORE

Fridell, Ron. *Sports Technology.*
Minneapolis: Lerner Publications, 2009.

Slade, Suzanne. *Basketball: How it Works.*
Mankato, Minn.: Capstone Press, 2010.

Tomecek, Stephen M. *Sports.*
New York: Chelsea House, 2010.

Yancey, Diane. *Basketball.*
Detroit: Lucent Books, 2011.

INTERNET SITES

FactHound offers a safe, fun way to find Internet sites related to this book. All of the sites on FactHound have been researched by our staff.

Here's all you do:

Visit *www.facthound.com*

Type in this code: 9781429699563

Super-cool stuff!

Check out projects, games and lots more at
www.capstonekids.com

INDEX

3D video, 44, 45

accelerometers, 6
apps, 42–43
arenas, 36, 37, 39, 40, 41, 44
autologous chondrocyte
    implantation (ACI),
    26, 27

backboards, 28–29, 33
basketballs, 5, 6–7, 22
Biasone, Danny, 33
breakaway rims, 29
broadcasting, 43, 44, 45

cameras, 22, 23, 30, 34, 35,
    38,39, 40, 45
cartilage, 26, 27
cloning, 26
coaches, 9, 12, 23, 31
computers, 7, 13, 24, 25, 34

data, 7, 13, 22, 23, 35, 37, 45
defibrillators, 11

electrocardiograms
    (EKGs), 11
Evans, Brooke, 27

fans, 36, 37, 38, 39, 40, 41,
    42, 43, 44, 45

goals, 12, 13
grip liquid, 16–17

gyroscopes, 6

hands, 16, 18–19
heart-rate belts, 13

Ikpah, Sessoter, 11
injuries, 12, 17, 26, 27, 28
instant replays, 4, 30–31,
    33, 36
Internet, 39, 44

Jennings, Brandon, 4
Jordan, Michael, 21
LEDs (Light Emitting
    Diodes), 33, 37
Lewis, Reggie, 10

Marchlinski, Francis, 11
medical screenings, 10–11
metal detectors, 38, 39
muscles, 10, 11

Naismith, James, 5

overseas broadcasts, 44

passing, 9, 18, 19, 23
playoffs, 34
Podoloff, Maurice, 33
practice, 6, 7, 8–9, 11, 12,
    13, 21, 24–25
"propulsion" shoes, 15

referees, 22, 30, 31, 32,
    33, 43
rims, 29, 33
Rose, Derrick, 4
rules, 5, 31, 43

scoreboards, 36–37, 40, 41
security, 38–39
sensors, 7
shoes, 5, 14–15, 16–17
shooting, 6–7, 8–9, 23,
    32–33, 34
shooting machines, 8–9
shot clocks, 33
simulations, 24–25
slam dunks, 14, 28–29
statisticians, 34, 35
stats, 34, 35, 36, 43
sweat, 18–19

"tattle texting," 39

tracking systems, 22–23,
    40–41
traction, 16–17
training, 8, 12–13, 24

uniform, 20–21

video, 30–31, 35, 36,
    39, 45
video screens, 30,
    36–37, 41